ADELE 25

UKULELE

ISBN 978-1-4950-5970-4

7777 W. BLUEMOUND RD. P.O. BOX 13819 MILWAUKEE, WI 53213

Hello

Words and Music by Adele Adkins and Greg Kurstin

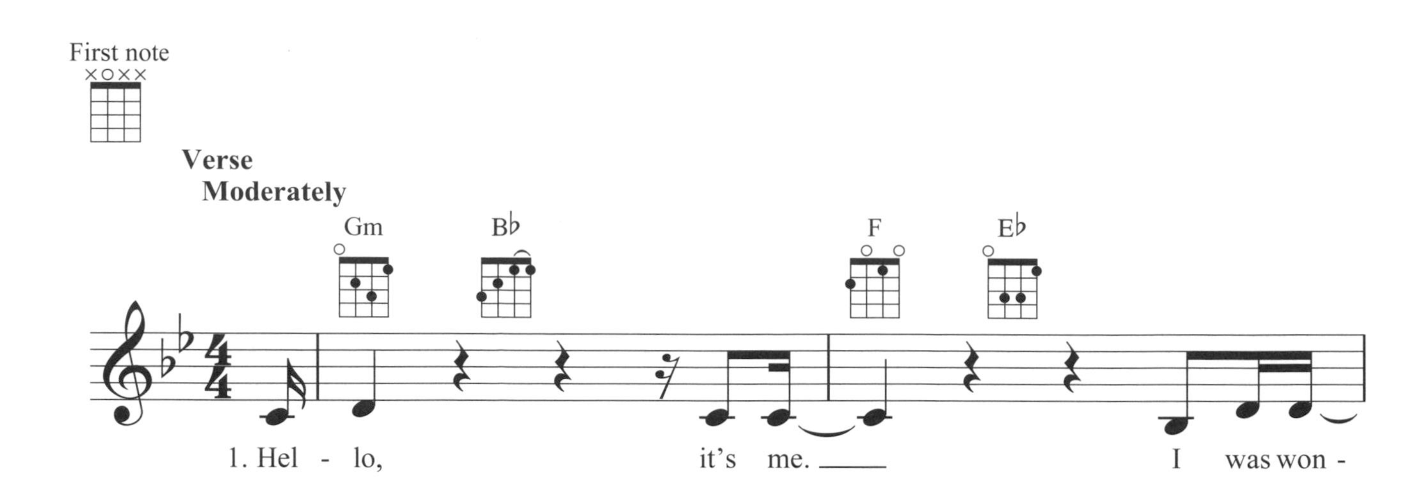

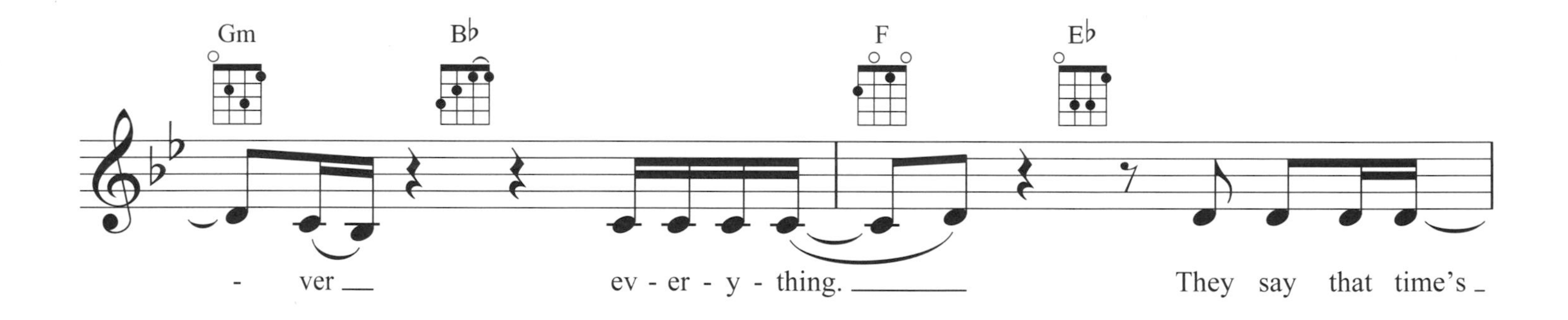

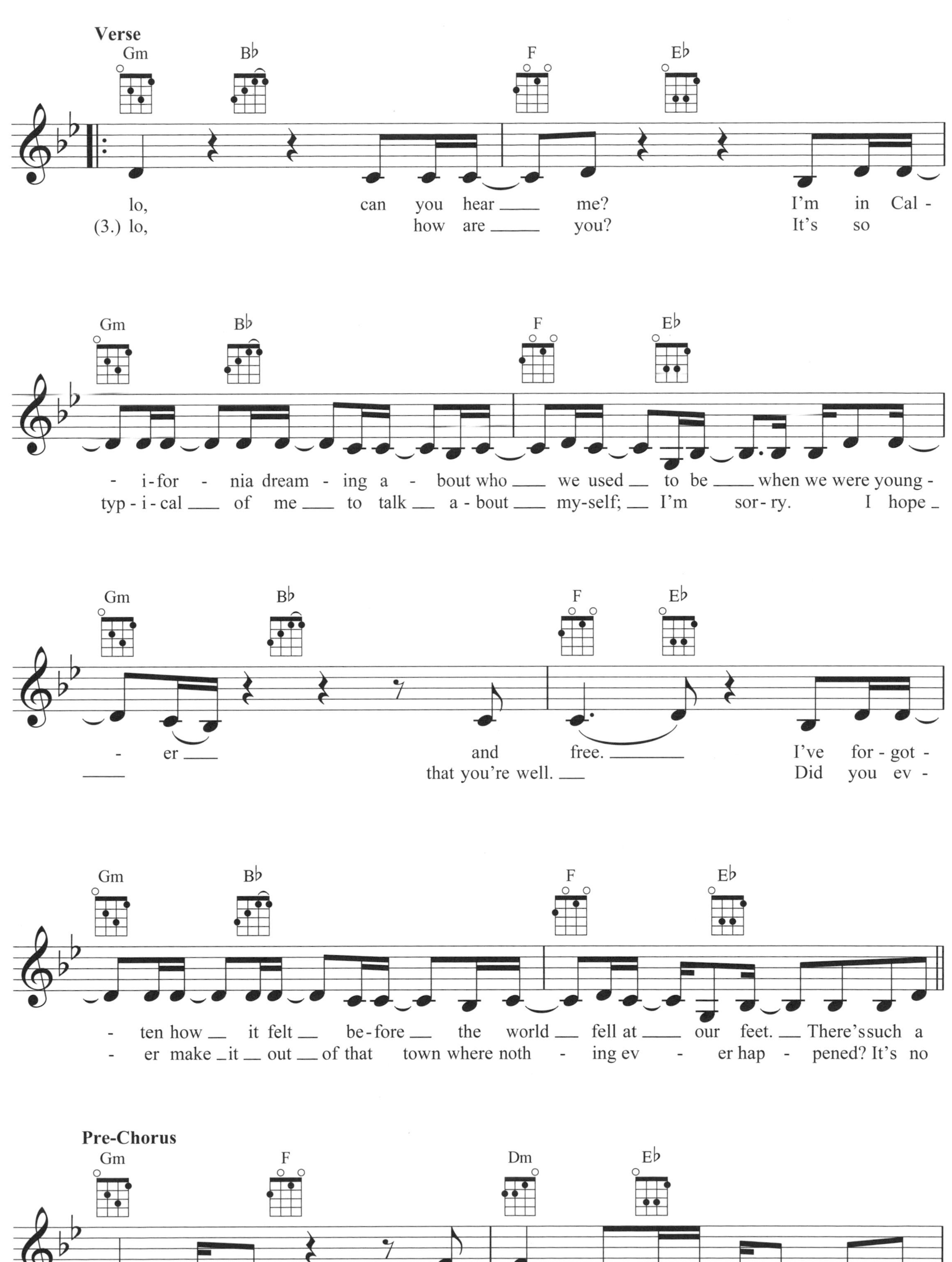
Verse
Gm
B♭
F
E♭
lo, can you hear me? I'm in Cal-
(3.) lo, how are you? It's so
Gm
B♭
F
E♭
-i-for-nia dream-ing a-bout who we used to be when we were young-
typ-i-cal of me to talk a-bout my-self; I'm sor-ry. I hope
Gm
B♭
F
E♭
-er and free. I've for-got-
that you're well. Did you ev-
Gm
B♭
F
E♭
-ten how it felt be-fore the world fell at our feet. There's such a
-er make it out of that town where noth-ing ev-er hap-pened? It's no
Pre-Chorus
Gm
F
Dm
E♭
dif-f'rence be-tween us, and a
se-cret that the both of us are

Chorus
Gm
F
E♭
Gm
E♭
mil - li - on miles.
run - ning out of time.
So:
Hel - lo from the oth - er side.
B♭
F
Gm
E♭
B♭
F
I must have called a thou - sand times
to tell you
Gm
E♭
B♭
F
I'm sor - ry for ev - 'ry - thing that I've done,
but when I call
Gm
E♭
B♭
F
Gm
you nev - er seem to be home.
Hel - lo from the out - side.
B♭
F
Gm
E♭
At least I can say that I've tried
B♭
F
Gm
E♭
to tell you
I'm sor - ry for

B♭
F
Gm
E♭
To Coda
breaking your heart. But it don't matter: it clearly doesn't
1.
tear you apart anymore.
3. Hel-
2.
Interlude
tear you apart anymore.
(Vocal ad lib.)
D.S. al Coda
Coda
tear you apart anymore.

Send My Love
(To Your New Lover)

Words and Music by Adele Adkins, Max Martin and Shellback

Bm
you ___ and me. ___ Mm, ___ that was what you told me.
down. ___ Mm, ___ there's on - ly one ___ way down.
Pre-Chorus
D
I'm giv - ing you ___ up, ___ I've for - giv - en it ___ all. ___
Bm
___ You set me ___ free. ___
Chorus
D
Send my love to your new lo - ov - er, ___ treat her bet - ter. ___ We've
Bm
got - ta let go of all of our ghosts; ___ we both know we ain't kids no more. ___
D
Send my love to your new lo - ov - er, ___ treat her bet - ter. ___ We've

Bm
To Coda
got - ta let go of all of our ghosts; _
we both know we ain't kids no more. ___
1.
D
2.
Bridge
D
If you're read - y, ___ if you're read - y, ___
if you're read - y, ___ I'm read - y. ___
Bm
If you're read - y, ___ if you're read - y, ___
we both know we ain't kids no more. ___
D
No, ___ we ain't kids no
Bm
more. ___

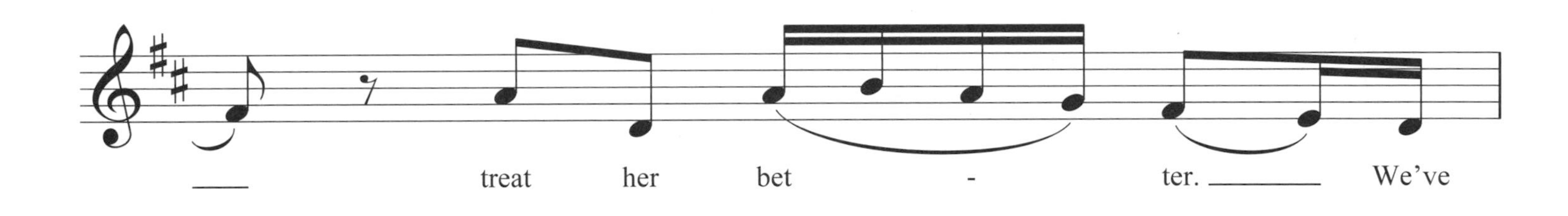

N.C.

we both know we ain't kids no more.

I Miss You

Words and Music by Adele Adkins and Paul Epworth

bod - y stand - ing o - ver me.
you and me set - ting the tone.
Ba - by, don't let the lights go

Pre-Chorus
Gm7
F6
down.
Ba - by, don't let the lights go down.

Cm7
Ba - by, don't let the lights go down, lights go down, lights go down, lights go down, lights go

down, down, down. I
Chorus
Gm7
F6
miss you when the lights go out; it il - lu - mi - nates all

Cm7
of my doubts. Pull me in, hold me tight,

Gm7
don't let go, ba - by, give me light. I miss you when the

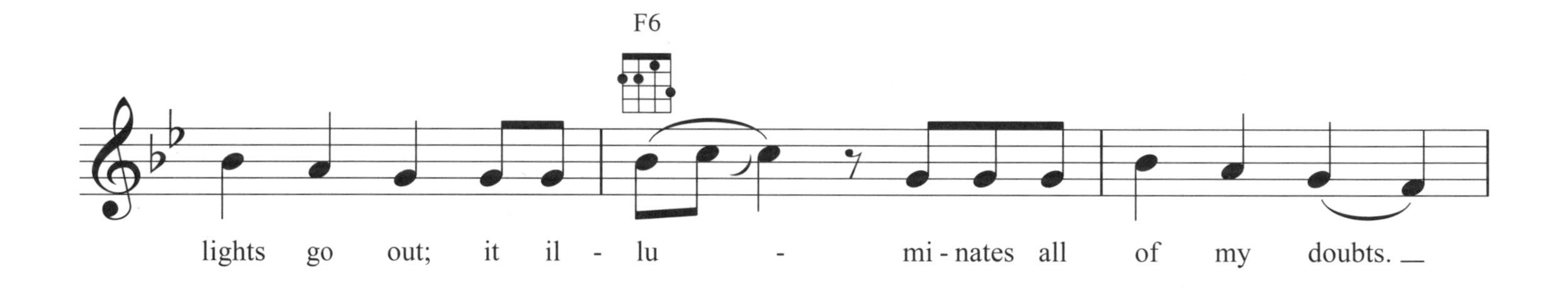
F6
lights go out; it il - lu - mi - nates all of my doubts.

Cm7
To Coda
Pull me in, hold me tight, don't let go, ba - by,

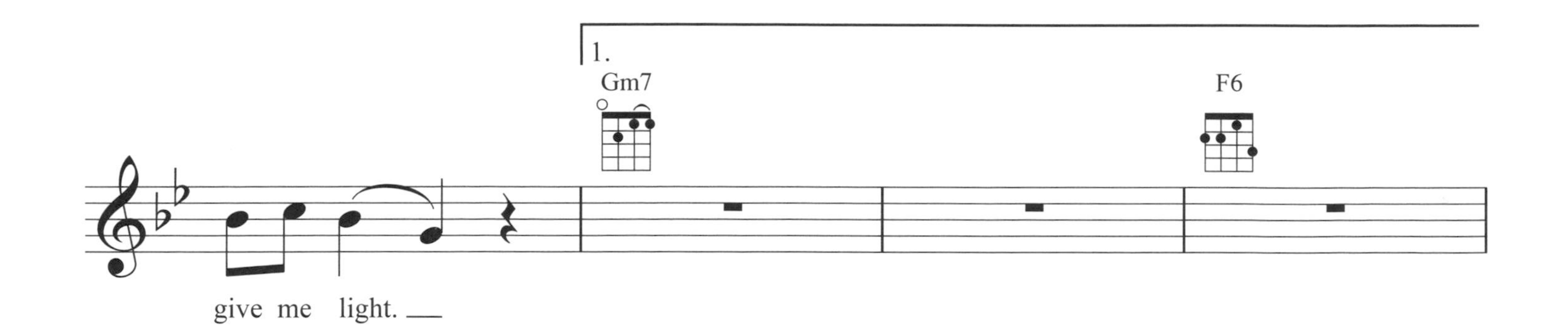
1.
Gm7
F6
give me light.

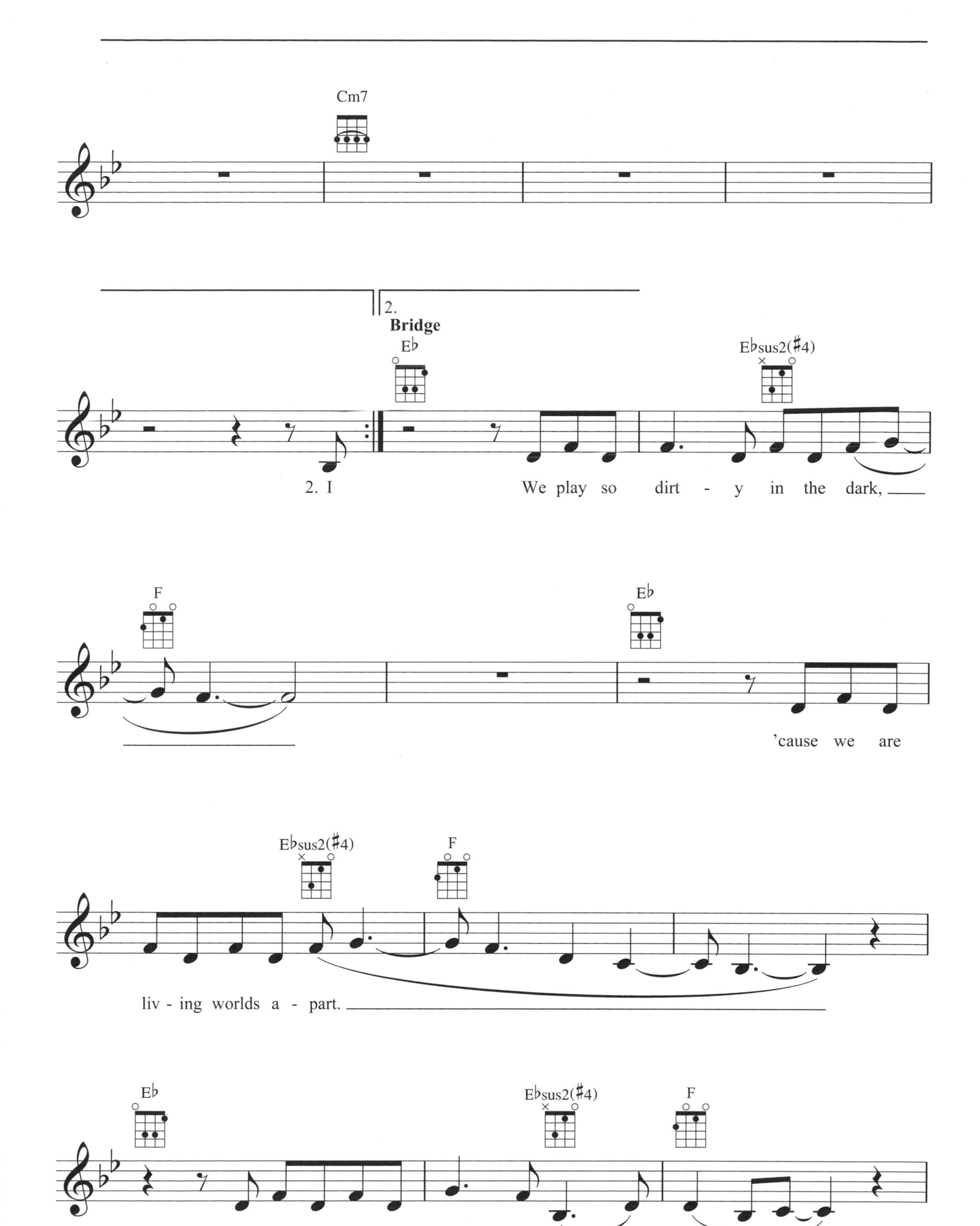
Cm7
2.
Bridge
E♭
E♭sus2(♯4)
2. I
We play so dirt - y in the dark,
F
E♭
'cause we are
E♭sus2(♯4)
F
liv - ing worlds a - part.
E♭
E♭sus2(♯4)
F
It on - ly makes it hard - er, ba - by.

E♭
E♭sus2(♯4)
It on - ly makes it hard - er, ba - by, hard - er, ba - by,
F
N.C.
D.S. al Coda
hard - er, ba - by. I
Coda
give me light. I
Outro
Gm7
F6
miss you. I miss you.
Cm7
I miss you. I
1.
2.
Gm7
miss you. I

When We Were Young

Words and Music by Adele Adkins and Tobias Jesso Jr.

B♭ F Gm7
lone, can I have a mo - ment be - fore I
fears; no - bod - y told ___ me that you'd be
F Dm F
go? ___ 'Cause I've been by my - self all night ___
here. And I swear you moved o - ver -
B♭ F Gm7
___ long, ___ hop - ing you're some - one ___ I used to ___
- seas; ___ that's what you ___ said ___ when you left ___
Pre-Chorus
C7sus4 C7 B♭ C7
know. ___ You look like a mov - ie, you sound like a song. ___
me. ___ You still look like a mov - ie, you still sound like a song. ___
Am7 B♭ C7
My god, this re - minds ___ me of when we were young. ___
Chorus
Am7 C7 F Am7
Let me pho - to - graph you in ___ this light, ___ in case ___

B♭
C7
F
Am7
it is the last time that we might be ex - act - ly like we were

B♭
C7
Dm7
F
To Coda
be - fore we re - al - ized we were sad of get - ting old. It made us rest -

B♭
B♭m
Gm7
3
- less. It was just like a mov - ie, it was just like a

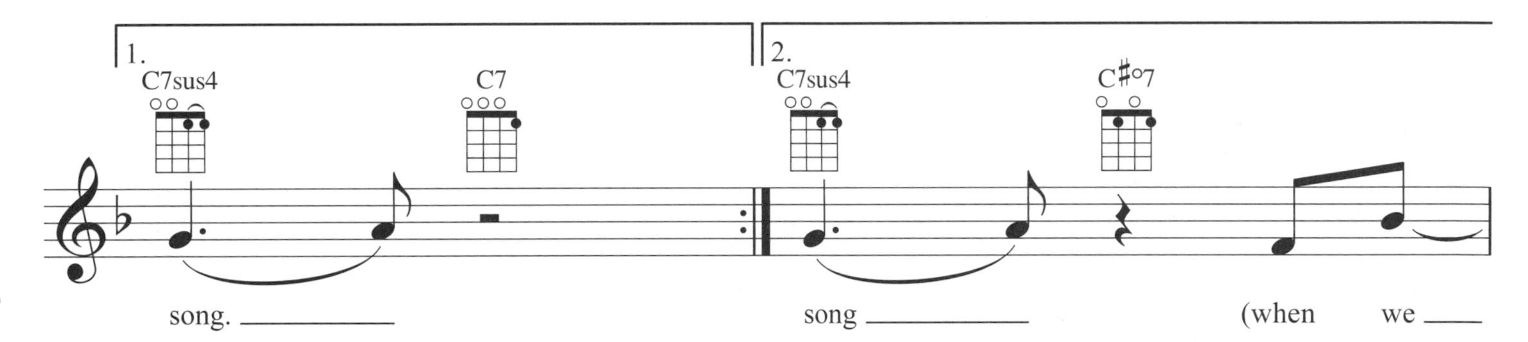
1.
C7sus4
C7
2.
C7sus4
C♯°7
song. song (when we

Dm
F
B♭
Fadd9
were young, when we were young, when we

Gm7
C7sus4
C♯°7
were young, when we were young.) It's hard

Bridge
Dm F B♭ Fadd9
to ad - mit that ev - 'ry - thing just takes me back to when you

Gm7 C7sus4 C♯°7
were there, to when you were there. And a part

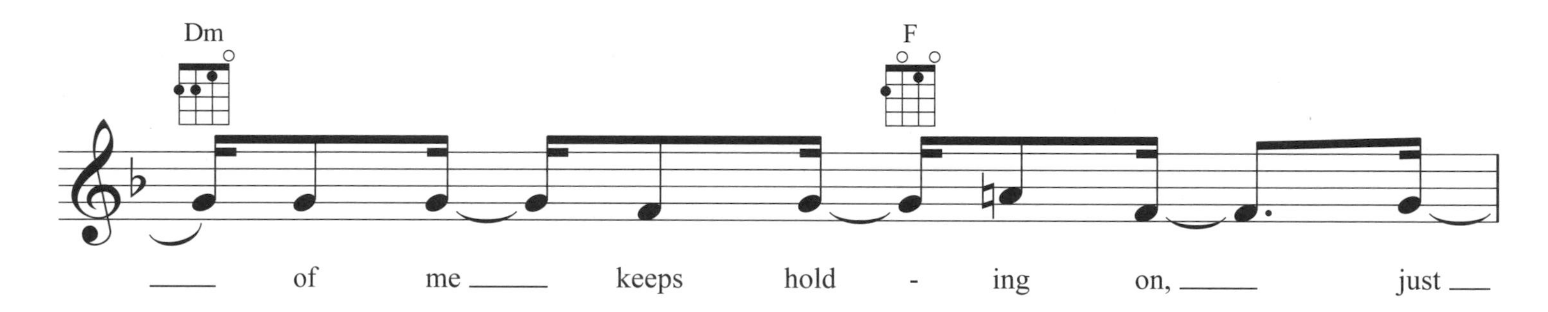
Dm F
of me keeps hold - ing on, just

B♭ Fadd9 Gm7
in case it has - n't gone. I guess I still care. Do

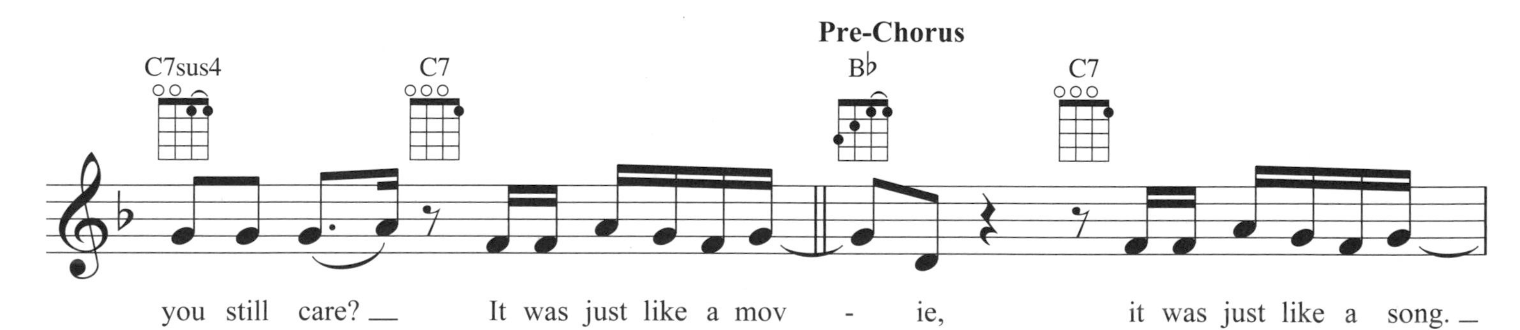
Pre-Chorus
C7sus4 C7 B♭ C7
you still care? It was just like a mov - ie, it was just like a song.

Am7 B♭ C7
My god, this re - minds me of when we were young.

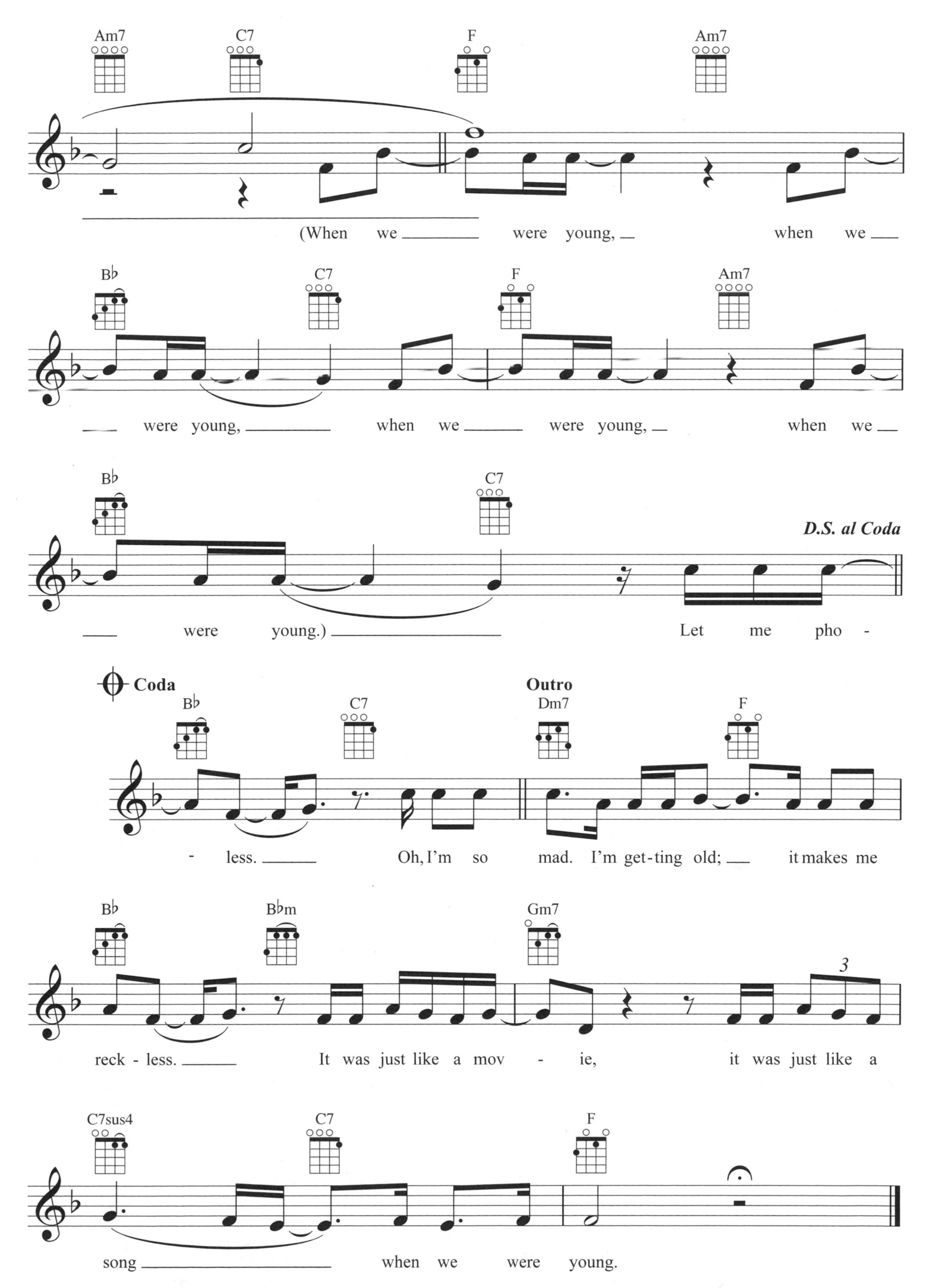
Am7
C7
F
Am7
(When we were young, when we
B♭
C7
F
Am7
were young, when we were young, when we
B♭
C7
D.S. al Coda
were young.) Let me pho -
Coda
Outro
B♭
C7
Dm7
F
- less. Oh, I'm so mad. I'm get-ting old; it makes me
B♭
B♭m
Gm7
3
reck - less. It was just like a mov - ie, it was just like a
C7sus4
C7
F
song when we were young.

Remedy

Words and Music by Adele Adkins and Ryan Tedder

Em7
D
Asus4
A
fore my eyes I saw; my
love, it is my truth, and
Em7
D
A
heart, it came to life. This ain't
I will al - ways love you,
Play 1st time only
G
A/G
4fr
G
eas - y; it's not meant to be. Ev - 'ry sto - ry has its
love you. When the
Chorus
D
Asus4
A
scars. But when the pain cuts you deep, and when the
Em
Bm
D
night keeps you from sleep - ing, just look and you will
Asus4
A
G
A
see that I will be your rem - e - dy. When the

D
Asus4
A
Em7
world seems so cruel and your heart makes you feel like a
Bm
D
Asus4
A
fool, I prom - ise you will see that I will
G
To Coda
N.C.
be, I will be your rem - e - dy.
1.
Em7
D
A
Em7
D
2.
Interlude
A
Em7
D
A
Oh,
Em7
D
A
Em7
D

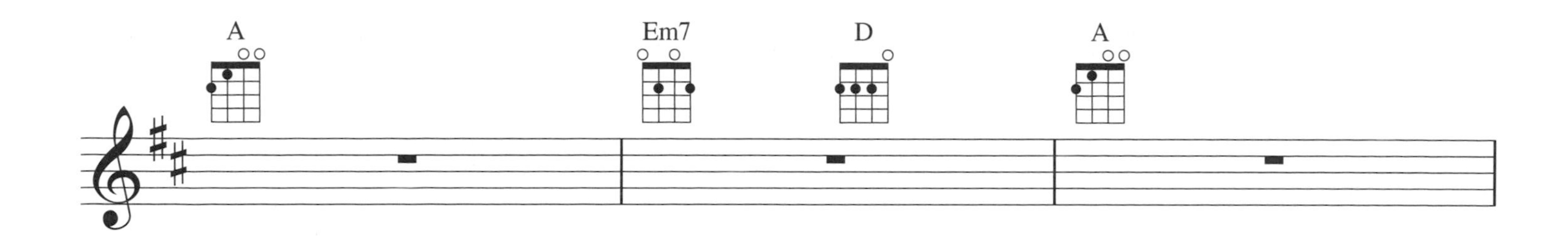
A
Em7
D
A

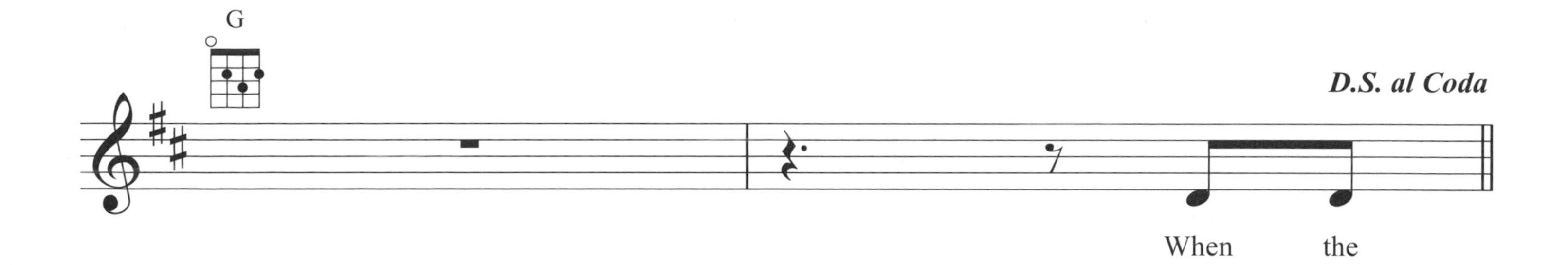
G
D.S. al Coda
When the

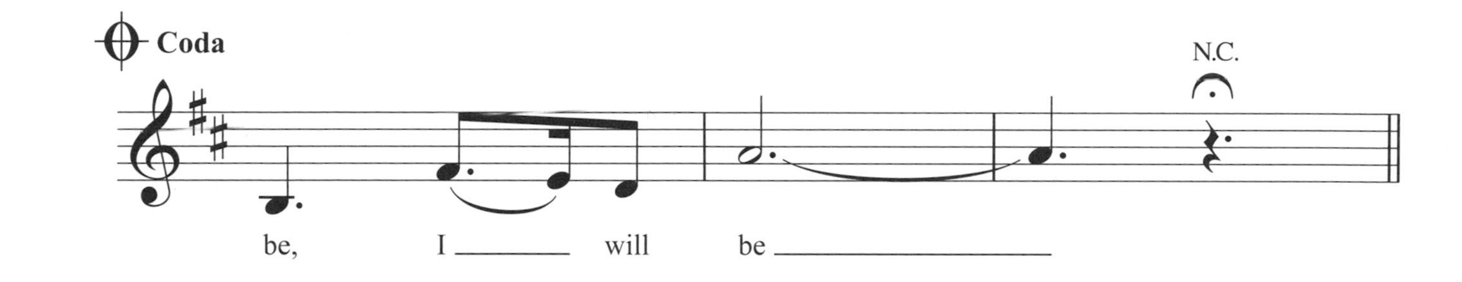
Coda
N.C.
be, I will be

Outro
Em7
D
A
your rem - e - dy.

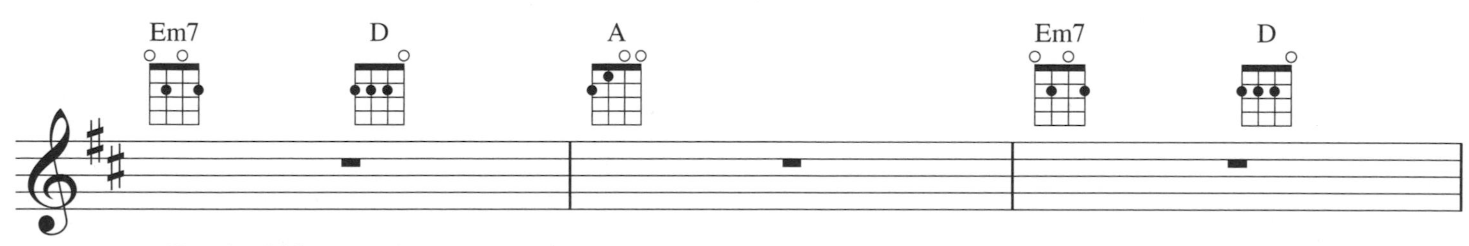
Em7
D
A
Em7
D
Vocal ad lib.

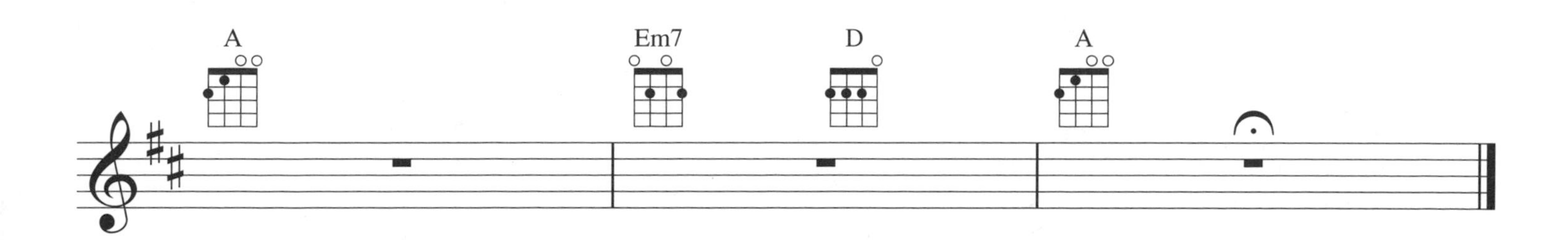
A
Em7
D
A

Water Under the Bridge

Words and Music by Adele Adkins and Gregory Kurstin

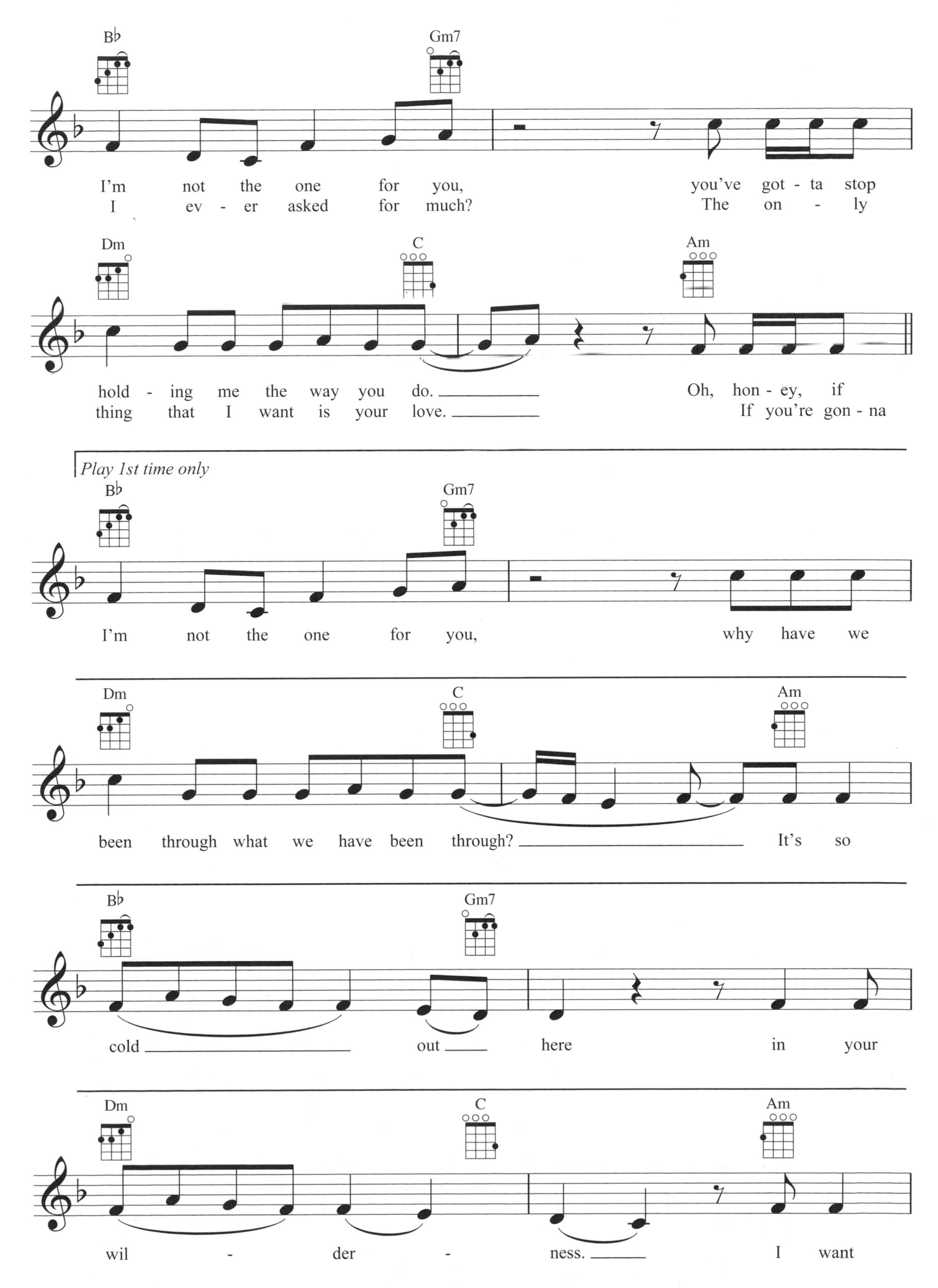

B♭
Gm7
I'm not the one for you, you've got - ta stop
I ev - er asked for much? The on - ly
Dm
C
Am
hold - ing me the way you do. Oh, hon - ey, if
thing that I want is your love. If you're gon - na
Play 1st time only
B♭
Gm7
I'm not the one for you, why have we
Dm
C
Am
been through what we have been through? It's so
B♭
Gm7
cold out here in your
Dm
C
Am
wil - der - ness. I want

B♭
Gm7
you ___ to be my keep - er, ___ but
Dm
C
not if you are so reck - less. ___ If you're gon - na
Chorus
F
Gm7
let me down, _ let ___ me down gen - tly. Don't pre - tend ___ that ___ you don't want me.
Dm
B♭
Our love ain't wa - ter un - der the bridge. ___ If ___ you're gon - na
F
Gm7
let me down, _ let ___ me down gen - tly. Don't pre - tend ___ that ___ you don't want me.
To Coda
Dm
B♭
Our love ain't wa - ter un - der the bridge. ___ Whoa. ___

F
Gm7

Say that

Dm
1.
B♭
our love ain't wa - ter un - der the bridge.

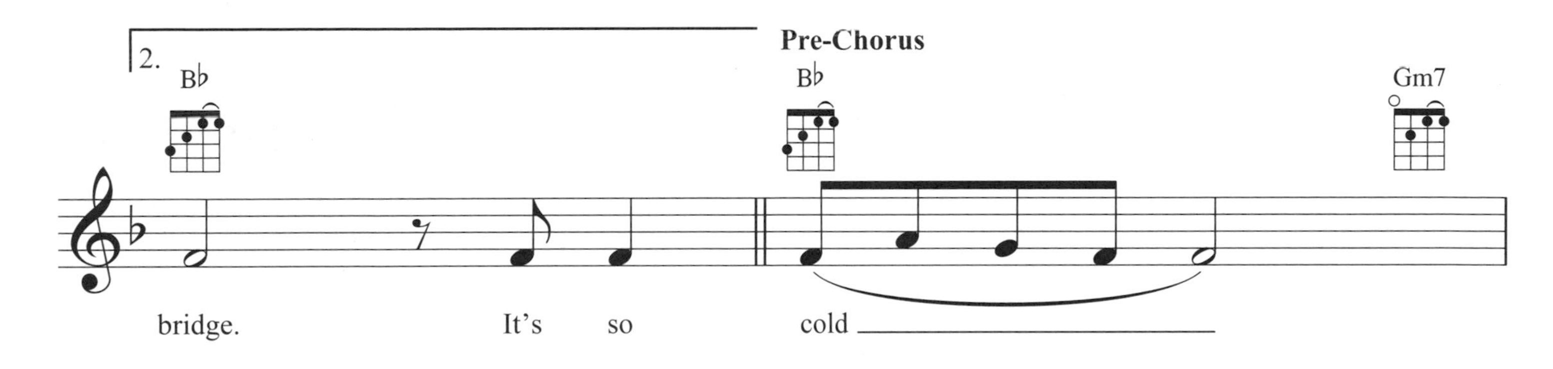
2.
B♭
Pre-Chorus
B♭
Gm7
bridge. It's so cold

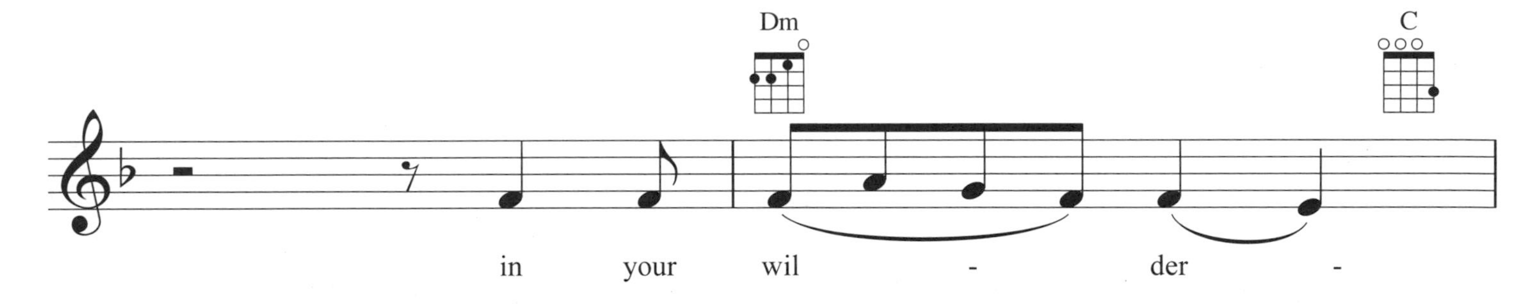
Dm
C
in your wil - der -

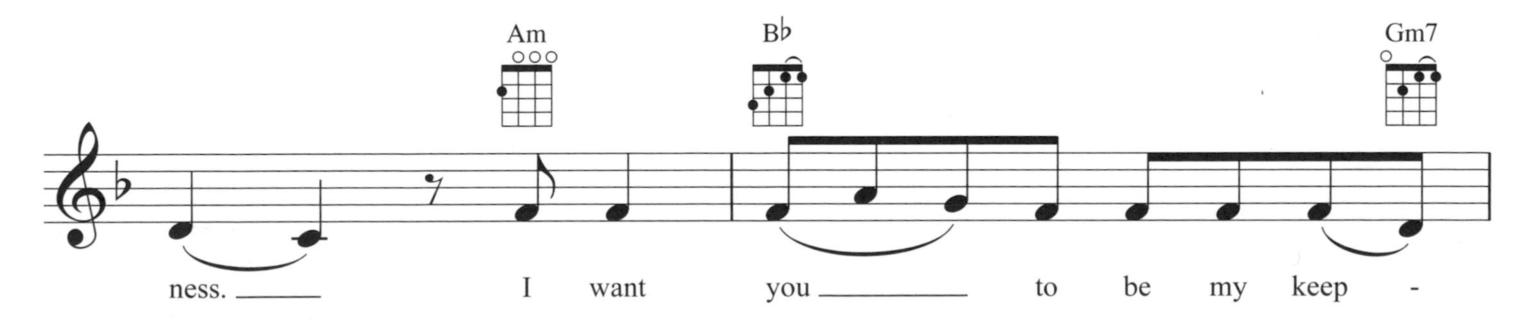
Am
B♭
Gm7
ness. I want you to be my keep -

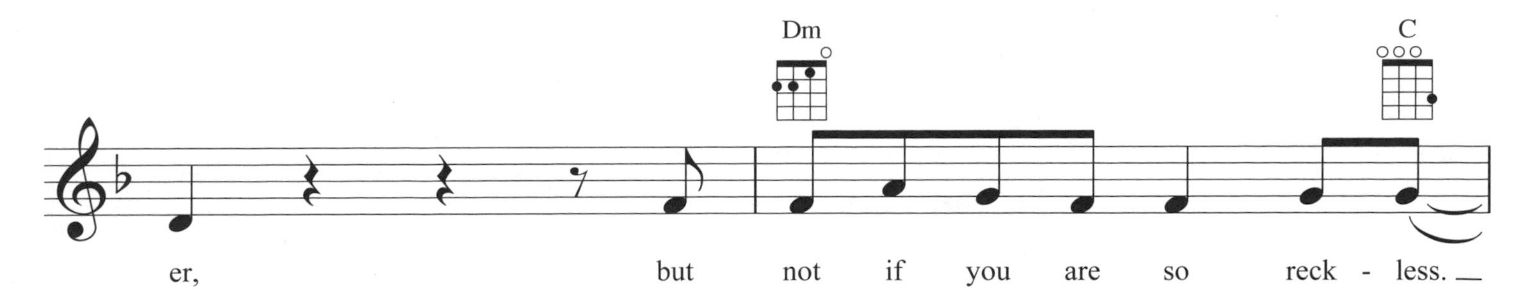
Dm
C
er, but not if you are so reck - less.

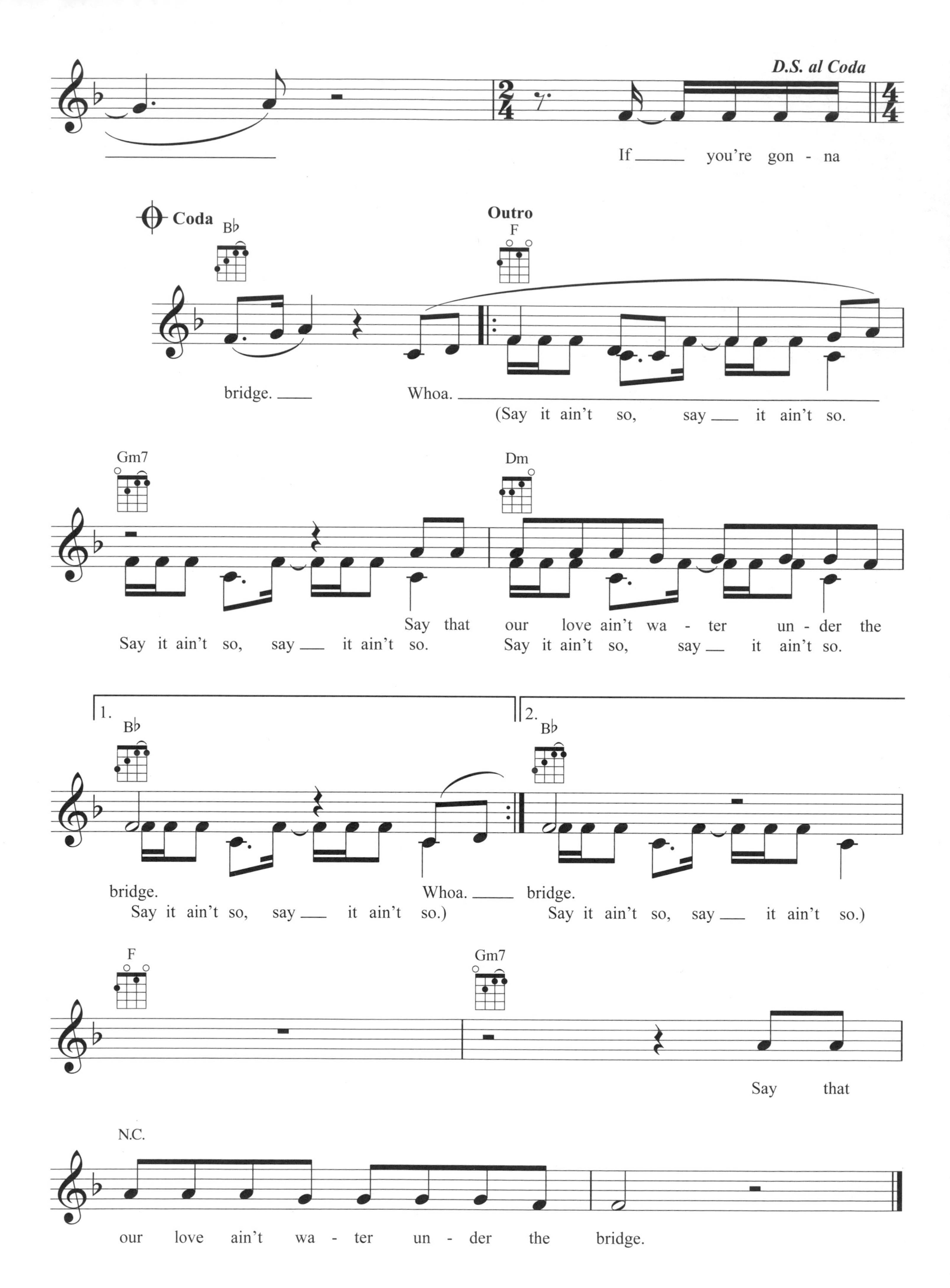
D.S. al Coda
If you're gon - na
Coda
Bb
Outro
F
bridge.
Whoa.
(Say it ain't so, say it ain't so.
Gm7
Dm
Say that our love ain't wa - ter un - der the
Say it ain't so, say it ain't so. Say it ain't so, say it ain't so.
1.
Bb
2.
Bb
bridge. Whoa. bridge.
Say it ain't so, say it ain't so.) Say it ain't so, say it ain't so.)
F
Gm7
Say that
N.C.
our love ain't wa - ter un - der the bridge.

Million Years Ago

Words and Music by Adele Adkins and Gregory Kurstin

* *Vocal sung an octave lower than written.*

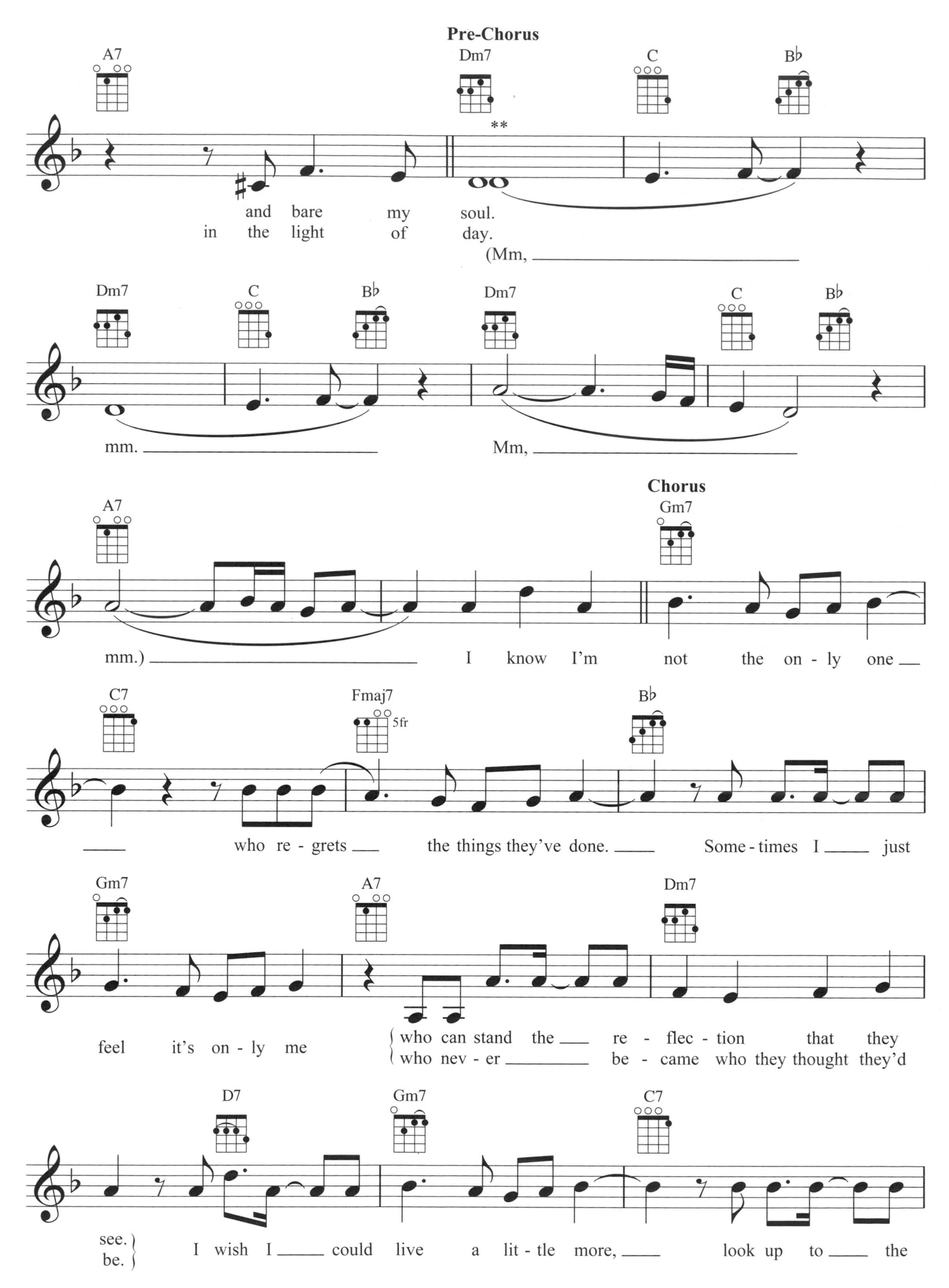

*** Vocal sung at written pitch.*

Fmaj7
5fr
B♭
Gm7
sky, not just the floor. I feel like my life is flash - ing by

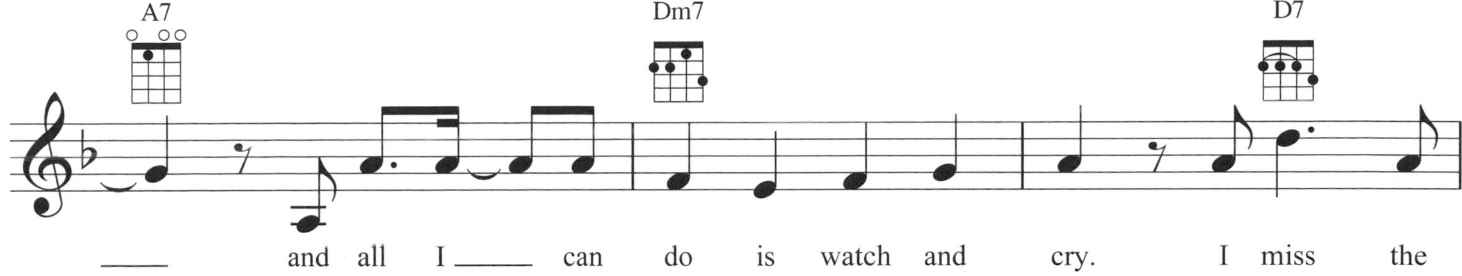
A7
Dm7
D7
and all I can do is watch and cry. I miss the

Gm7
C7
Fmaj7
5fr
3
air, I miss my friends, I miss my moth - er, I miss it when

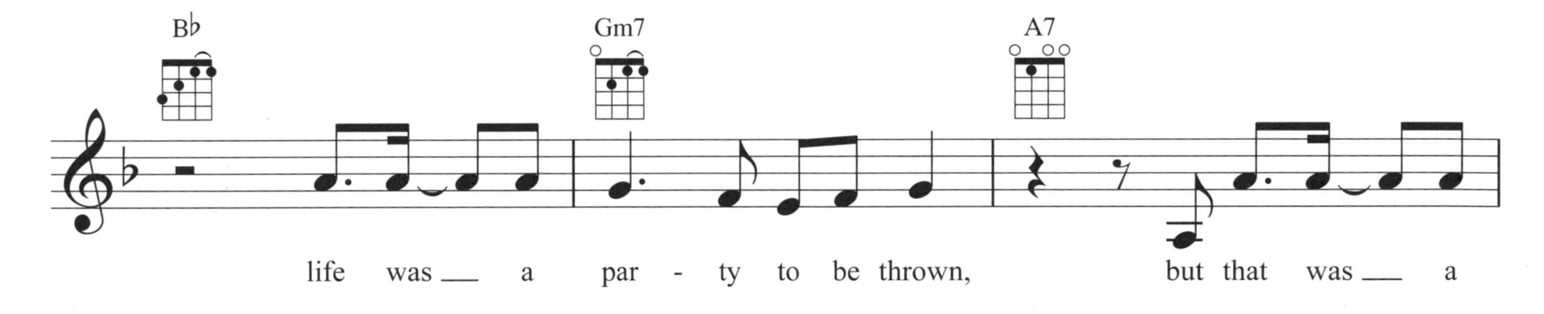
B♭
Gm7
A7
life was a par - ty to be thrown, but that was a

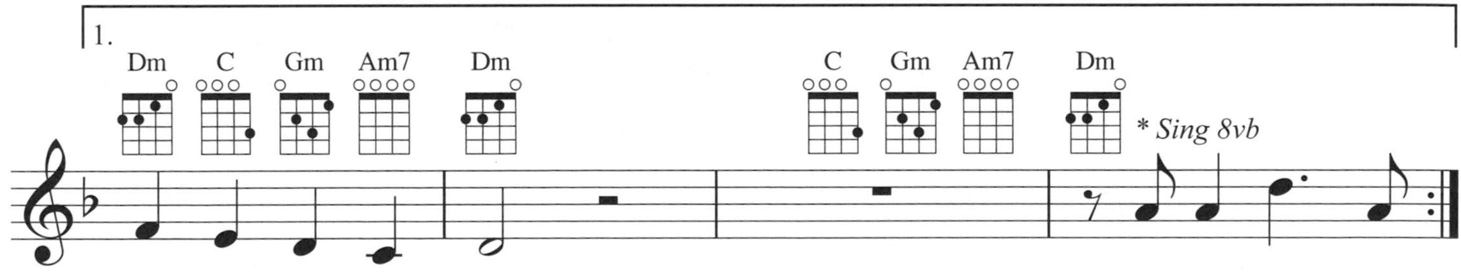
1.
Dm C Gm Am7 Dm
C Gm Am7 Dm
* Sing 8vb
mil - lion years a - go.
2. When I walk a -

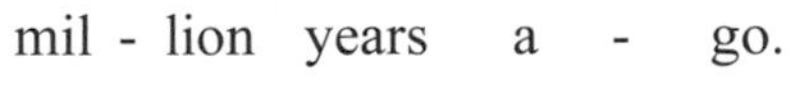
2.

Dm C Gm Am7 Dm
C Gm Am7 Dm
mil - lion years a - go, a mil - lion years a - go.

River Lea

Words and Music by Adele Adkins and Brian Burton

First note

Verse
Moderately

C D

1. Ev - 'ry - bod - y tells me it's 'bout time that I moved on, that I

Em D

need to learn to light - en up and learn how to be young. But

C D

my heart is a val - ley; it's so shal - low and man - made. I'm

Em D

scared to death if I let you in that you'll see I'm just a fake.

Verse

C D

2. Some - times I feel lone - ly in the arms of your touch, but I
3. I should prob - 'ly tell you now, be - fore it's way too late, that I

* *Vocal sung an octave lower than written.*

*** Vocal sung at written pitch.*

Chorus
Em
D
Em
D
roots, in my veins, in my blood, and I stain ev - 'ry heart that I use to heal the pain.
A
Em
D
Em
Oh, it's in my roots, in my veins, in my blood, and I stain ev - 'ry
D
A
heart that I use to heal the pain. So I blame it on the
Em
D
Em
Riv - er Lea, the Riv - er Lea, the Riv - er Lea. Yeah, I blame it on the
D
1.
A
Riv - er Lea, the Riv - er Lea, the Riv - er Lea.

2.
A
Em
D
Riv - er Lea. So I blame it on the Riv - er Lea, the Riv - er Lea, the
Em
D
Riv - er Lea. Yeah, I blame it on the Riv - er Lea, the Riv - er Lea, the
Outro
A
Em
D
Riv - er Lea. Riv - er Lea,
Em
D
Riv - er Lea, Riv - er Lea,

A
N.C.
2nd time, Fine
Riv - er Lea. Riv - er Lea, Riv - er Lea.

Love in the Dark

Words and Music by Adele Adkins and Samuel Dixon

Am
C
Em
I can't stay this time 'cause I don't love you an - y -
long - er we ig - nore it all, the more that we will
F
Pre-Chorus
Am
Cmaj7
more. Please stay where you are, don't come an -
fight. Please don't fall a - part; I can't face
Em7
F
Am
- y clos - er. Don't try to change my mind;
your break - ing heart. I'm try - ing to be brave;
Cmaj7
Em7
I'm be - ing cruel to be kind.
stop ask - ing me to stay.
Chorus
F
Fmaj7
5fr
G
I can't love you in the dark.
Am
Cmaj7
C
Fmaj7
5fr
It feels like we're o -

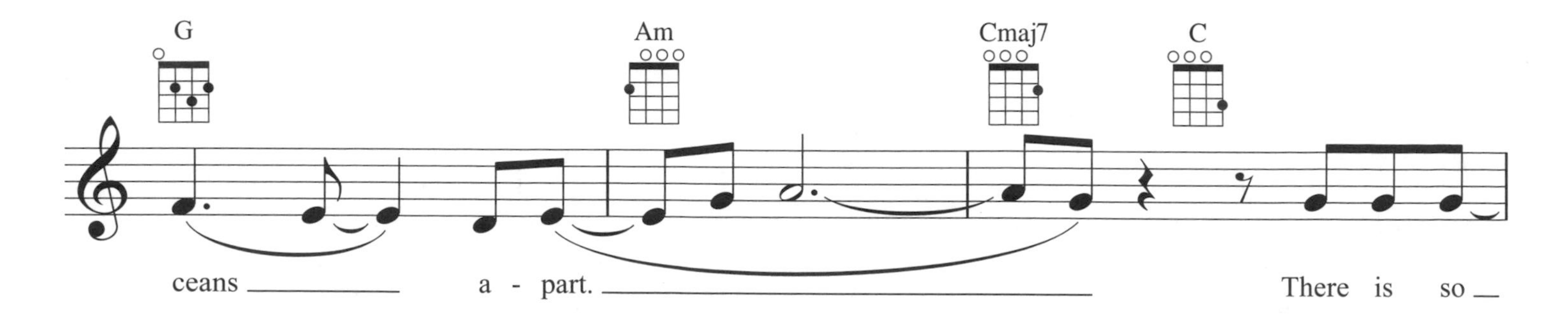
G
Am
Cmaj7
C
ceans a - part. There is so

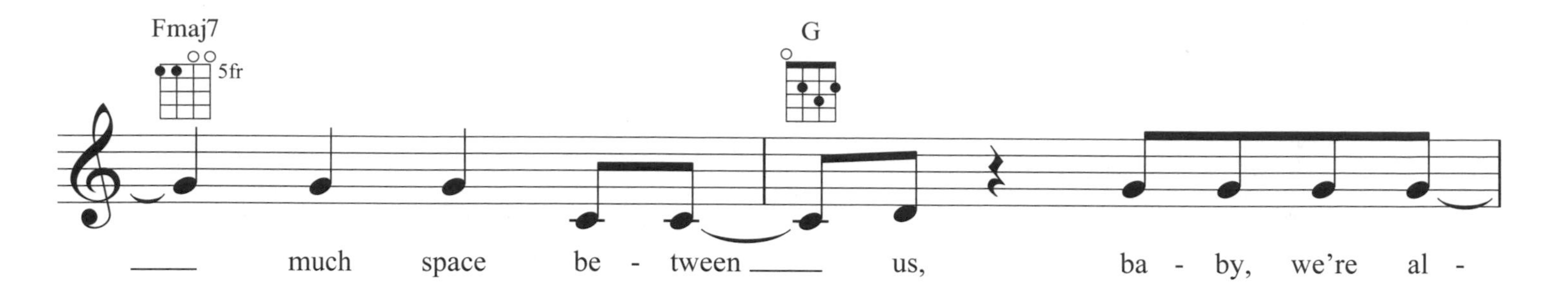
Fmaj7
5fr
G
much space be - tween us, ba - by, we're al -

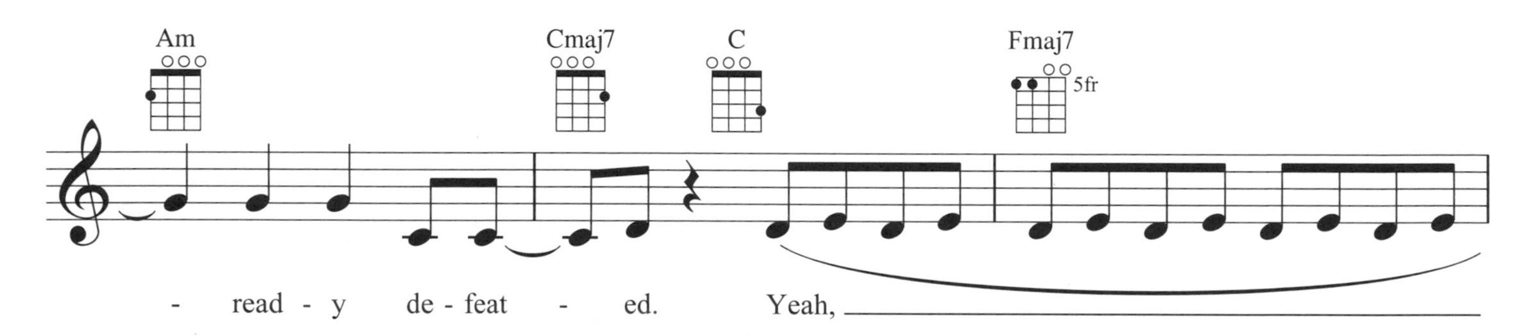
Am
Cmaj7
C
Fmaj7
5fr
- read - y de - feat - ed. Yeah,

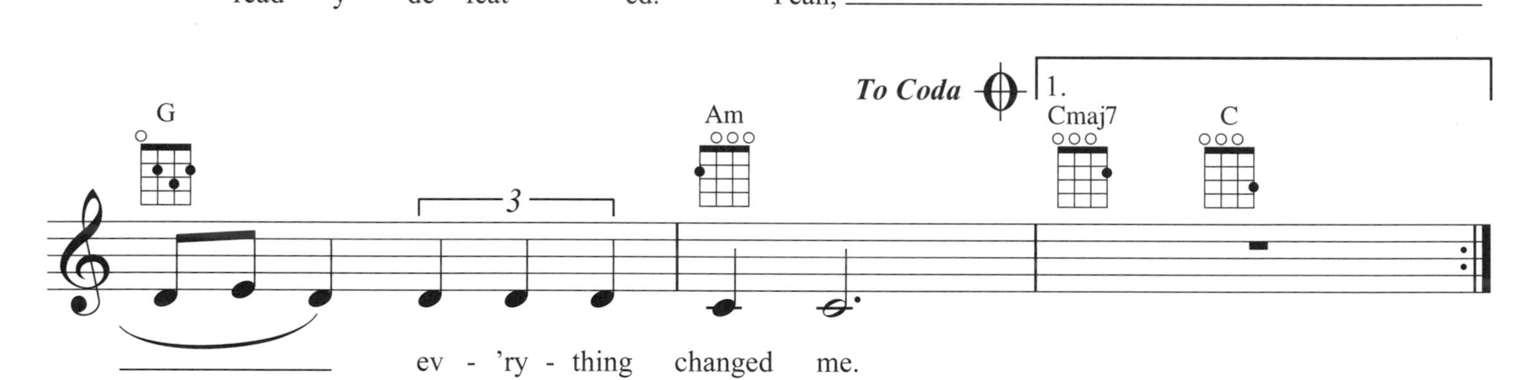
To Coda
1.
G
Am
Cmaj7
C
3
ev - 'ry - thing changed me.

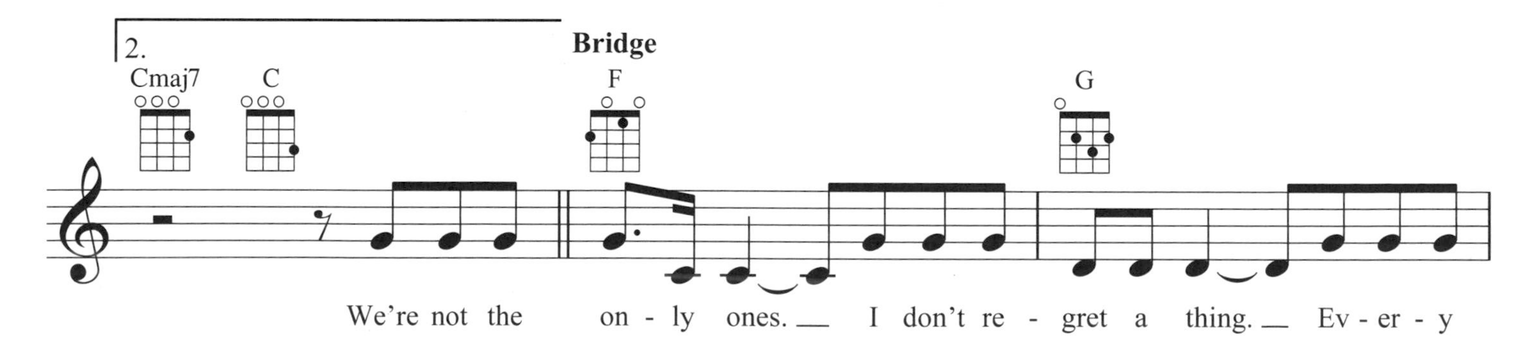
2.
Bridge
Cmaj7
C
F
G
We're not the on - ly ones. I don't re - gret a thing. Ev - er - y

Em7
Am
word I've said you know I'll al - ways mean. It is the

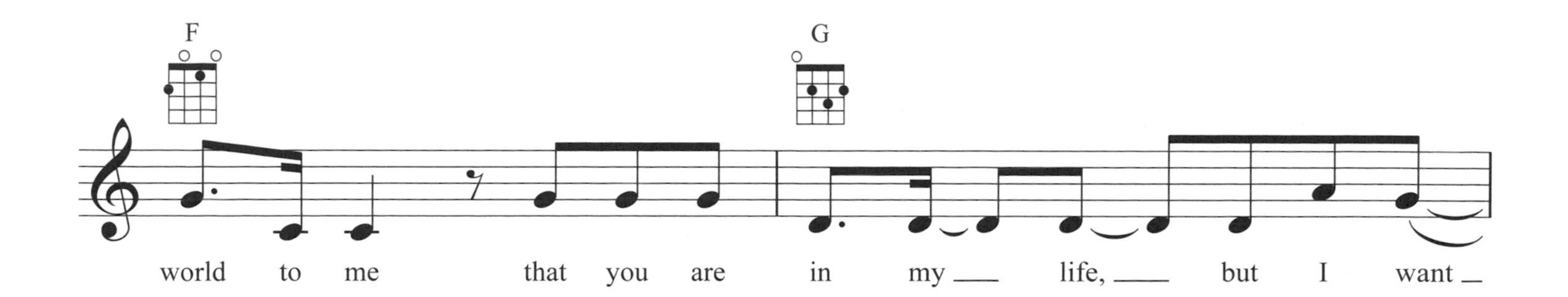
F
G
world to me that you are in my life, but I want

Am/D
to live and not just sur - vive.

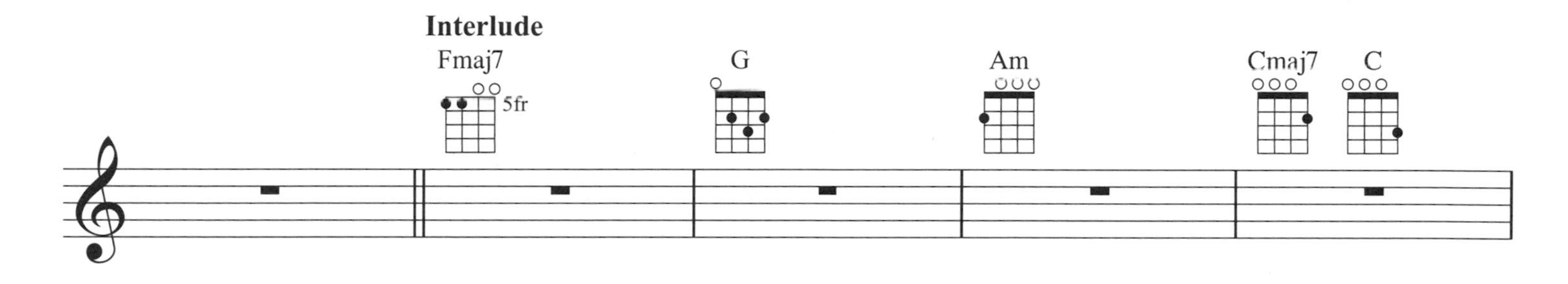
Interlude
Fmaj7
5fr
G
Am
Cmaj7
C

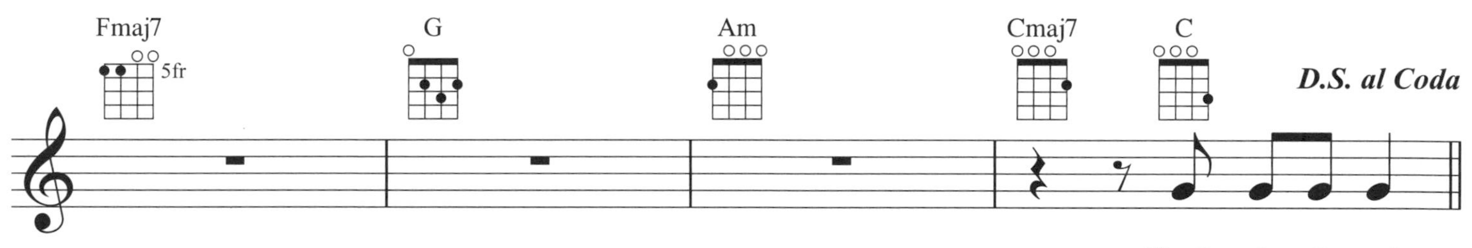
Fmaj7
5fr
G
Am
Cmaj7
C
D.S. al Coda
That's why I can't

Coda
Cmaj7
C
Outro
Fmaj7
5fr
And I

G
Am
don't think you can save me.

All I Ask

Words and Music by Adele Adkins, Philip Lawrence, Bruno Mars and Chris Brown

Am
just play pre - tend,
me like you do,
like we're not scared
and since you're the on -
B♭
C
of what is com - ing next or scared of hav - ing
- ly one that mat - ters, tell me: who do I run
Pre-Chorus
A
Dm
F
noth - ing left.
to?
Look, don't get me wrong; I know there
Gm
C7sus4
is no to - mor - row. All I
Chorus
F
D7
3
ask is: if this is my last
Gm
C7sus4
night with you, hold me like I'm more

C
F
D7
3
than just a friend.
Give me a mem - 'ry
Gm
C7sus4
I can use.
Take me by the hand
C
F
C
while we do what lov - ers
Dm
F
Gm
do. It mat - ters how this ends,
'cause
C7sus4
To Coda
1.
Fmaj7
5fr
what if I nev - er love a - gain?
(Instrumental)
2.
Bridge
F7
3
a - gain?
Let this be our

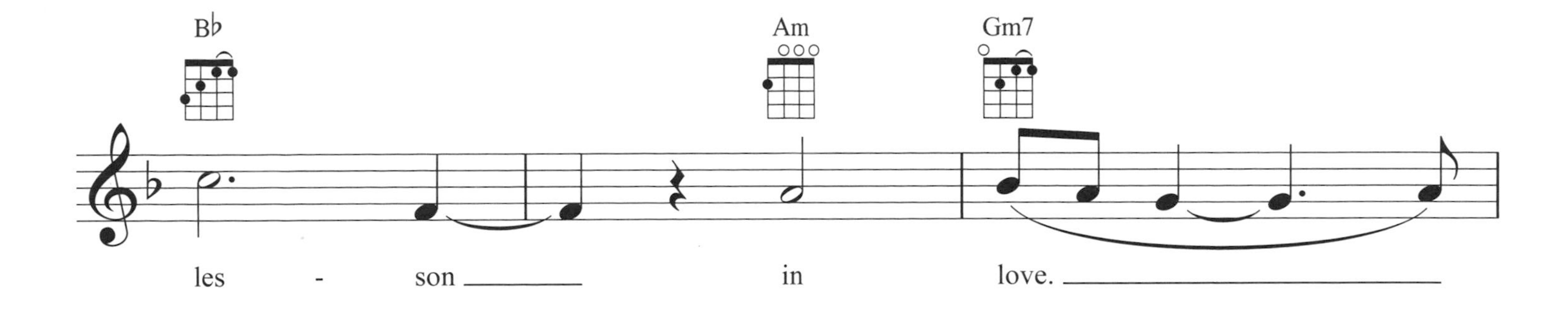
B♭
Am
Gm7
les - son in love.

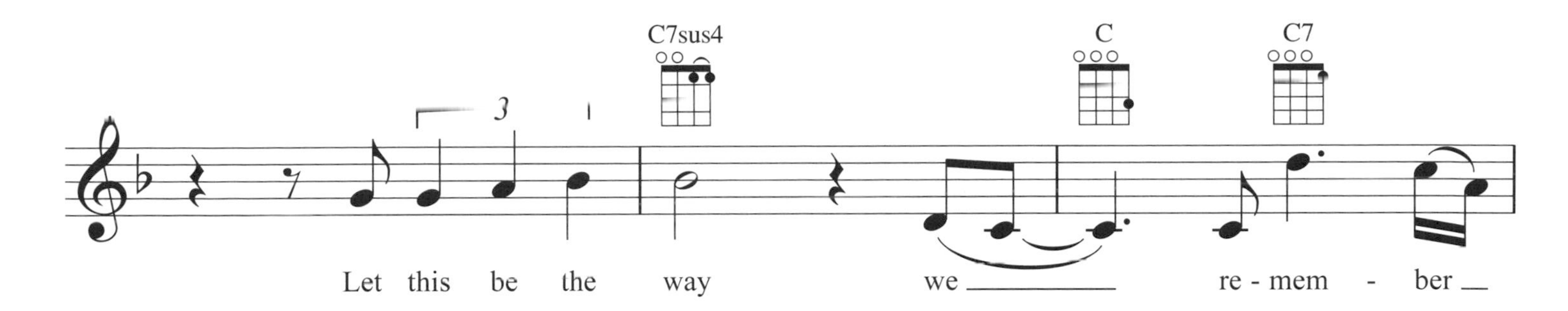
C7sus4
C
C7
3
Let this be the way we re - mem - ber

Am7
A
us. I don't wan - na be cruel or vi -

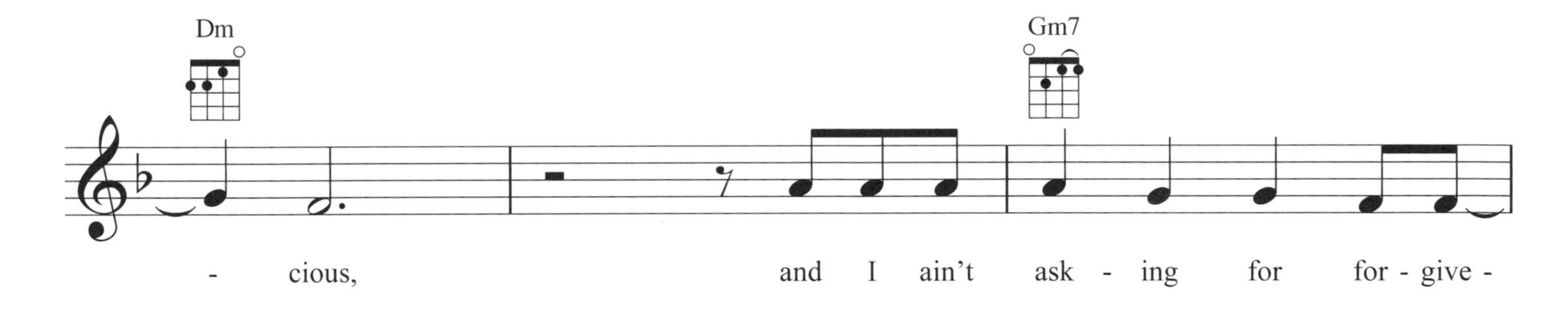
Dm
Gm7
- cious, and I ain't ask - ing for for - give -

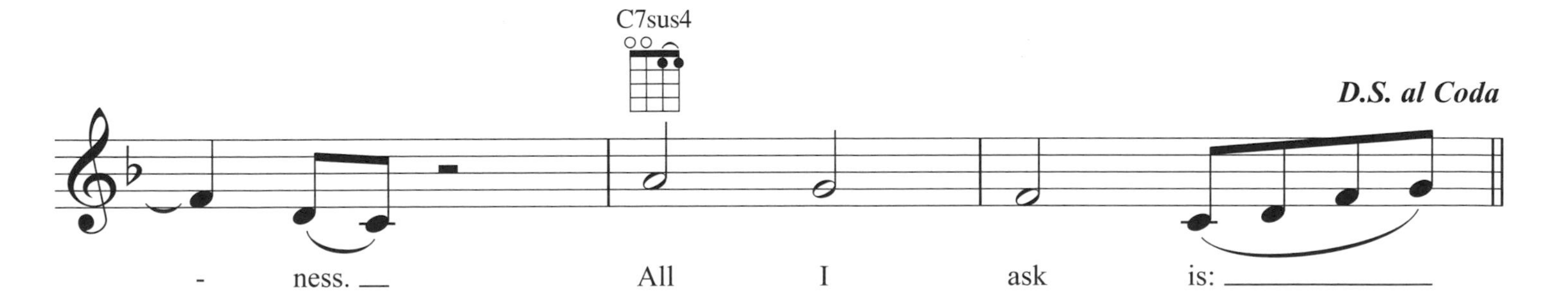
C7sus4
D.S. al Coda
- ness. All I ask is:

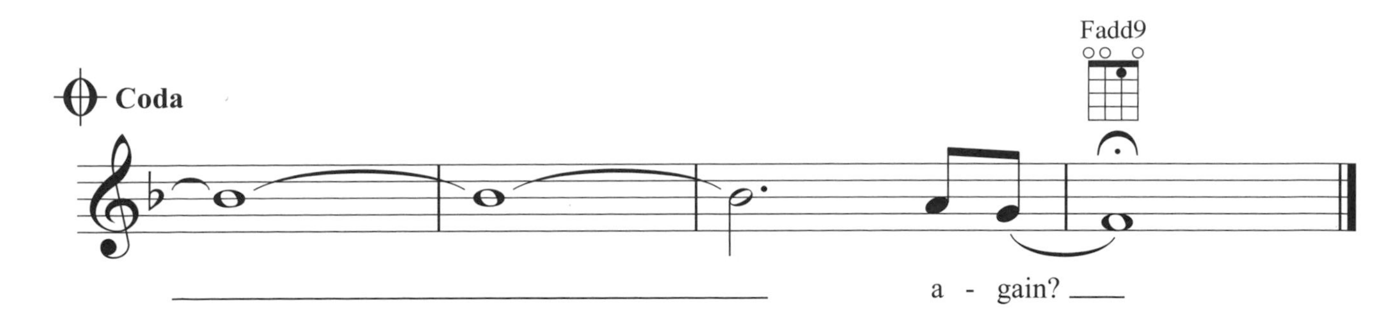
Coda
Fadd9
a - gain?

Sweetest Devotion
Words and Music by Adele Adkins and Paul Epworth
First note
Verse
Slowly, in 2
G
F
C
Pre-Chorus
1. With your lov - ing, there ain't noth - ing that
(2.) ev - er be what - ev - er you
I can't a - dore. The way I'm run - ning with you, hon - ey, means we can
want me to be. I'd go un - der and all o - ver for
break ev - 'ry law. I find it fun - ny that you're the on - ly one I
your clar - i - ty. When you won - der if I'm gon - na
nev - er looked for. There is some - thing in your lov - ing that
lose my way home, just re - mem - ber that, come what - ev - er, I'll be
tears down my walls.
yours all a - long.
I was - n't read - y then; I'm read - y now, I'm

F
C
G
head - ing straight for you. You will on - ly be e - ter - nal - ly the
Chorus
F
C
G
F
C
one that I be - long to. The sweet - est de - vo - tion
G
F
C
G
hit me like an ex - plo - sion. All of my life I've been
F
C
G
F
C
Em
fro - zen; the sweet - est de - vo - tion I know.
Interlude
G
F
C
G
1.
F
C
G
F
C
G
F
C
2.
F
C
2. I'll for -
I've been

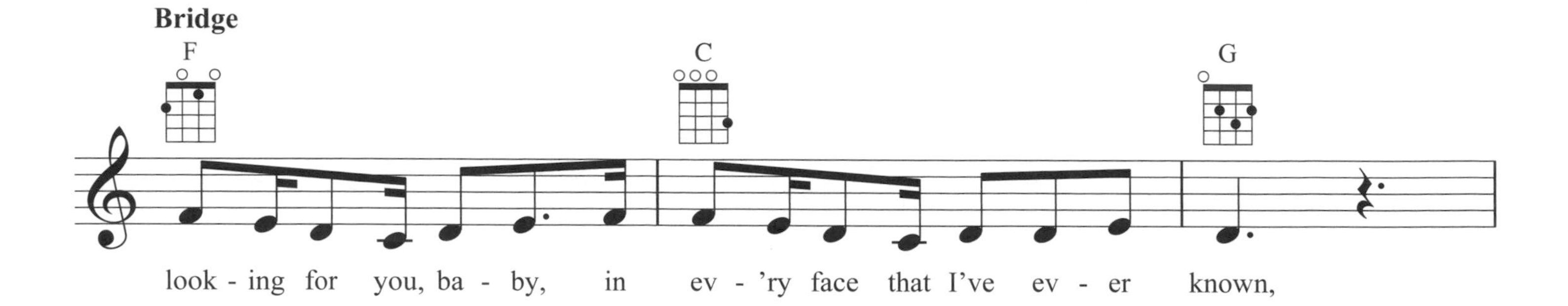
Bridge
F C G
look - ing for you, ba - by, in ev - 'ry face that I've ev - er known,

F C
and there is some - thing 'bout the way you love me that fi - nal - ly feels

G Em
like home. You're my light, you're my

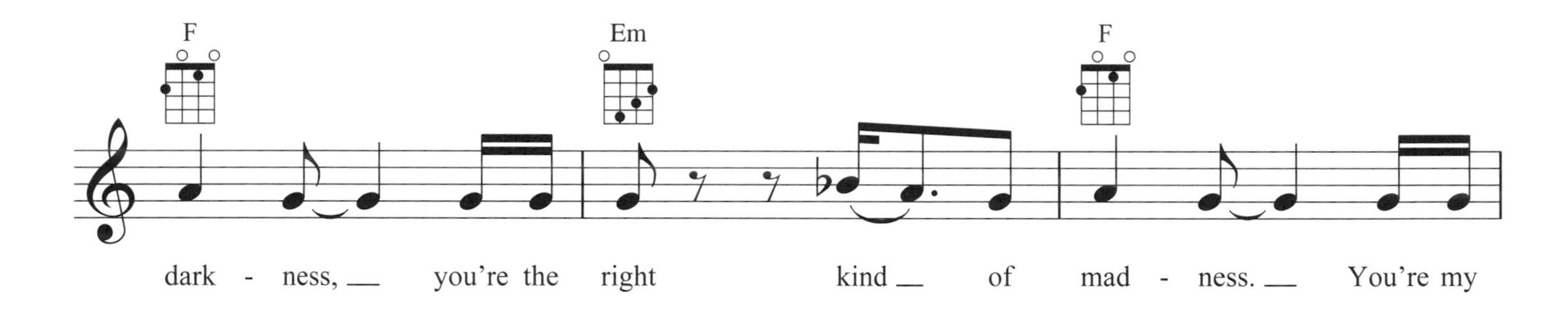
F Em F
dark - ness, you're the right kind of mad - ness. You're my

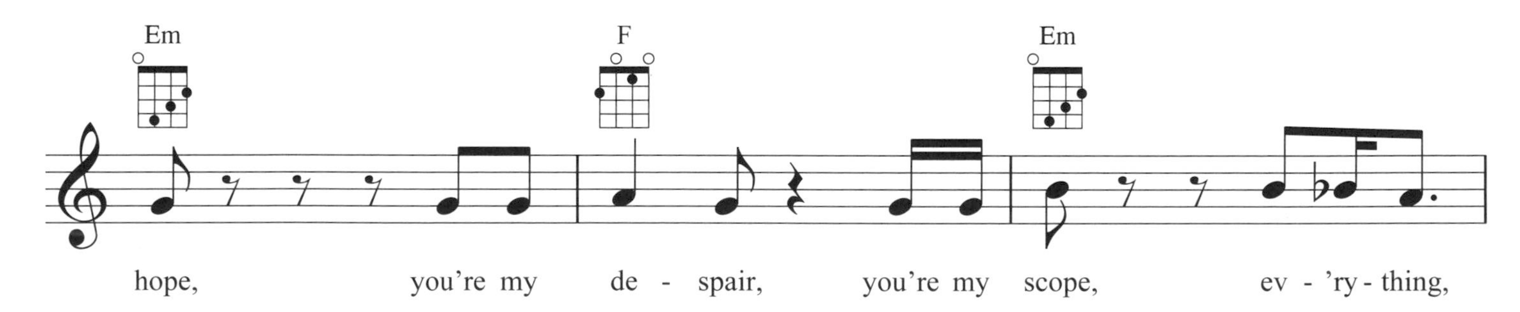
Em F Em
hope, you're my de - spair, you're my scope, ev - 'ry - thing,

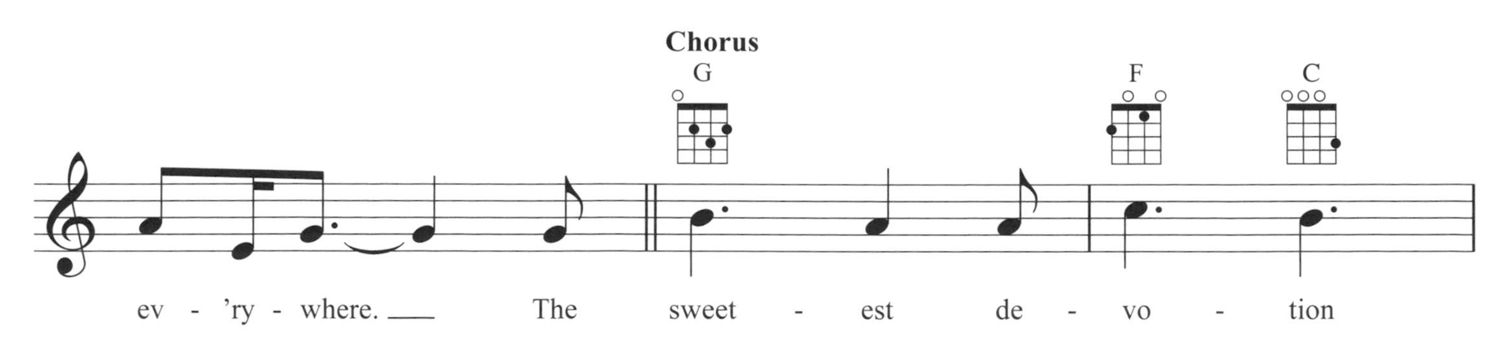
Chorus
G F C
ev - 'ry - where. The sweet - est de - vo - tion

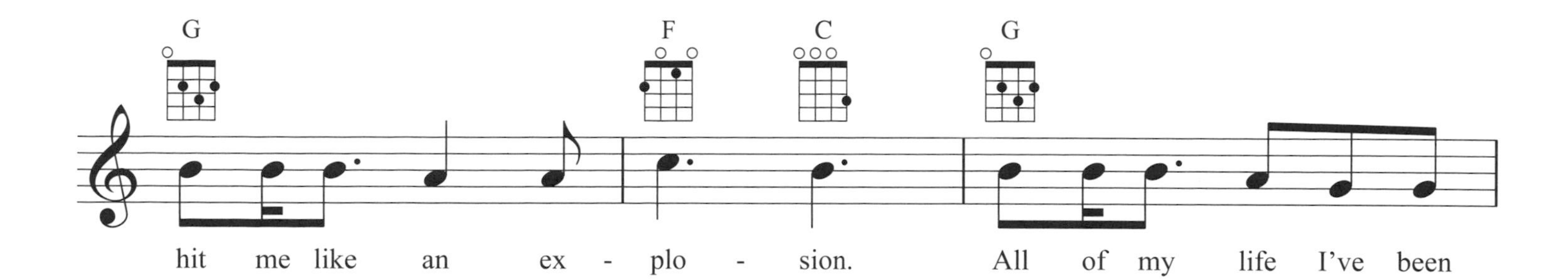
G F C G
hit me like an ex - plo - sion. All of my life I've been

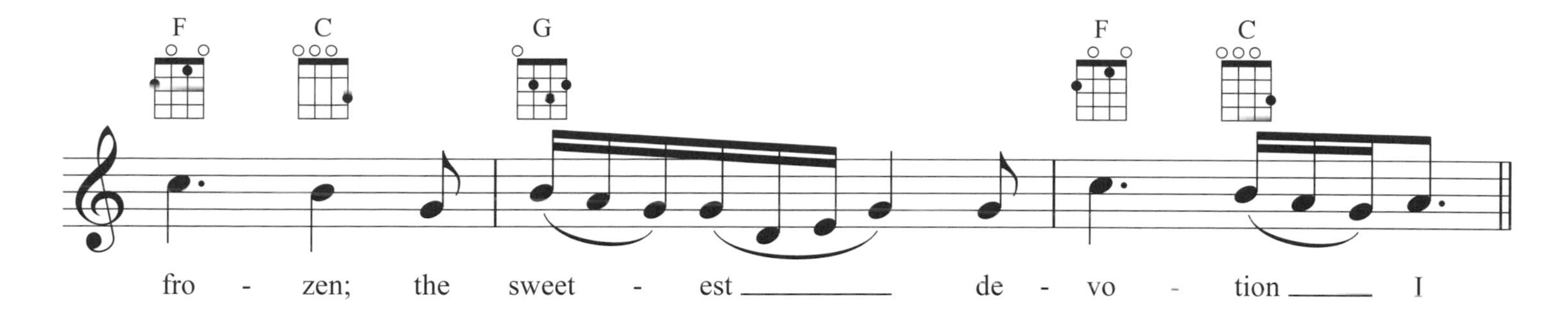
F C G F C
fro - zen; the sweet - est de - vo - tion I

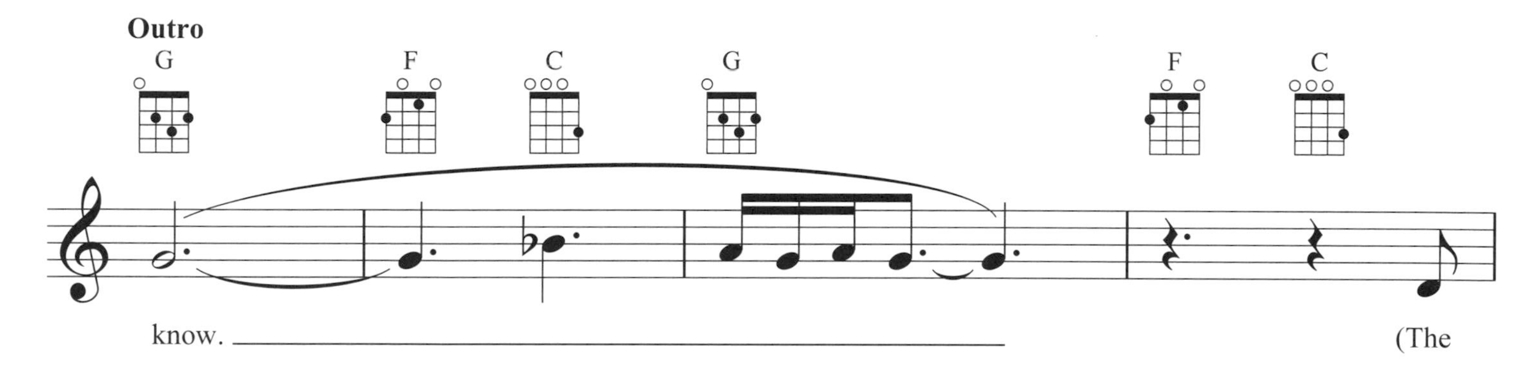
Outro
G F C G F C
know. (The

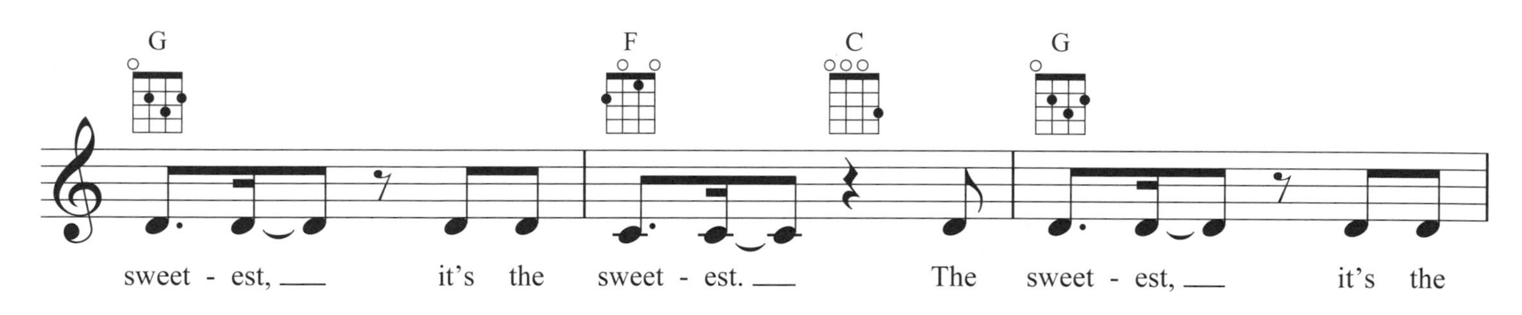
G F C G
sweet - est, it's the sweet - est. The sweet - est, it's the

F C G F C
sweet - est. The sweet - est, it's the sweet - est. The

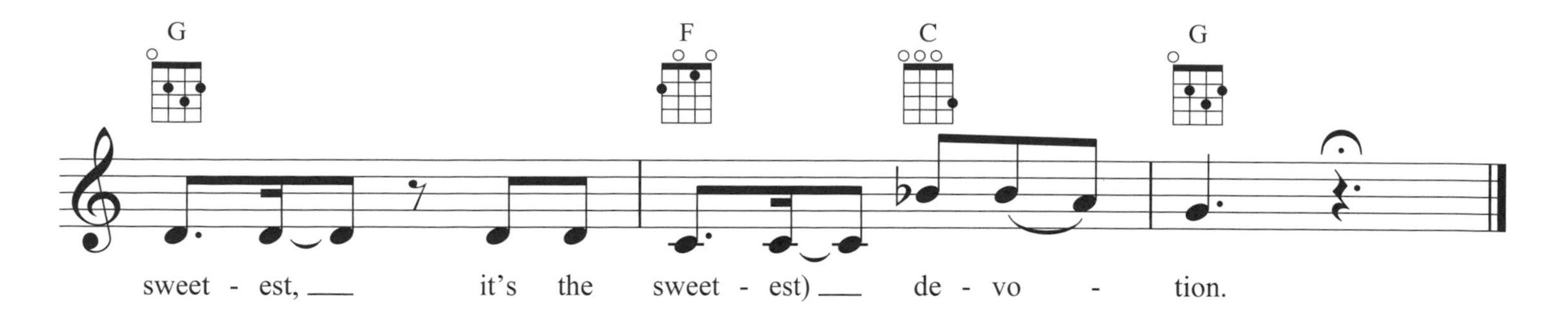
G F C G
sweet - est, it's the sweet - est) de - vo - tion.